Amigurumi
Animal Friends™

Cheepy Chick,
page 24

Frankie Frog,
page 21

Curious Cat,
page 7

Happy Dog,
page 10

Stinky Skunk,
page 14

Precious Pig,
page 27

Nutty Squirrel,
page 18

Teddy Bear,
page 5

Oliver Owl,
page 2

Oliver Owl

Design by Michele Wilcox

Skill Level
■■□□ EASY

Size
About 7 inches tall

Materials

- Worsted weight yarn: 2½ oz/125 yds brown and small amount each of gold, off-white and beige
- Size 6 (4mm) needles or size needed to obtain gauge
- Polyester fiberfill
- 6mm animal eyes (optional)

Gauge
14 sts and 24 rows = 4 inches/10cm in St st.
To save time, take time to check gauge.

Special Abbreviation
Knit in front and back (kfb): Inc 1 by knitting in front and back of next st.

Pattern Note
Instructions are given for knit eyes if animal is to be used by a young child.

Head
Beg at neck with brown, cast on 18 sts.

Row 1: Knit.

Row 2: Purl.

Row 3: Kfb in each st across—36 sts.

Row 4: Purl.

Rows 5–20: [Rep Rows 1 and 2] 8 times.

Row 21: [K2tog] across row—18 sts.

Row 22: Purl.

Row 23: Rep Row 21—9 sts.

Cut, leaving long end of yarn. Thread end into yarn needle, draw through all sts on needle, pull tight to secure. Sew back seam and stuff head. Do not sew neck opening.

Eye
Make 2

With off-white, cast on 3 sts.

Row 1: Kfb in each st across—6 sts.

Row 2: Rep Row 1—12 sts.

Row 3: *K1, kfb; rep from * across—18 sts.

Row 4: Knit.

Bind off. Shape into circle and sew seam. Sew in place on face, and then insert either purchased or knit eye.

Knit Eye
With brown, cast on 2 sts.

Row 1: Kfb in each st—4 sts.

Row 2: [K2tog] twice—2 sts.

Cut yarn leaving a long end. Thread end into yarn needle, draw end through both sts on needle and pull tight to secure. Gather around the edge of piece and pull tog.

Beak
With gold, cast on 6 sts.

Row 1: Knit.

Row 2: Purl.

Row 3: Knit.

Row 4: [P2tog] across—3 sts.

Cut, leaving long end of yarn. Thread end into yarn needle, draw through all sts on needle, pull tight to secure. Referring to photo, sew in place.

Ears
Cut 6 strands of 6-inch long brown yarn. Using 3 strands for each ear, make fringe knot on each side of head. Unravel strands of yarn and trim even.

Tummy
With beige, cast on 5 sts.

Row 1: Knit.

Row 2: Kfb in each st across—10 sts.

Rows 3–14: Knit.

Row 15: [K2tog] across—5 sts. Bind off.

Body

Beg at bottom of body, with brown, cast on 12 sts.

Row 1: Knit.

Row 2: Purl.

Row 3: Kfb of each st across—24 sts.

Row 4: Purl.

Row 5: *K3, kfb; rep from * across—30 sts.

Row 6: Purl.

Rows 7–20: Rep [Rows 1 and 2] 7 times.

Row 21: *K3, k2tog; rep from * across—24 sts.

Row 22: Purl.

Row 23: *K2, k2tog; rep from * across—18 sts.

Row 24: Purl.

Row 25: *K1, k2tog; rep from * across—12 sts.

Row 26: Purl.

Cut, leaving long end of yarn. Thread end into yarn needle, draw through all sts on needle, pull tight to secure. Sew back seam. Attach tummy. Stuff and sew bottom seam across. Fit neck of head over top of body and sew in place.

Foot
Make 2

With gold, cast on 5 sts for first toe.

Rows 1–3: Knit.

Row 4: Knit across, cast on 5 sts for 2nd toe—10 sts.

Row 5: Knit across 5 cast-on sts only; turn, leaving rem sts unworked.

Rows 6–8: K5. At end of Row 8, cast on 5 sts for 3rd toe.

Row 9: Rep Row 5.

Rows 10–12: K5.

Row 13: Knit across—15 sts.

Row 14: [K2tog] 7 times, k1—8 sts.

Row 15: Knit. Bind off.

Fold each toe in half and sew seams. Referring to photo, sew to body.

Tail

With brown, make 2 pieces same as for foot. Do not fold and sew toes. Holding the 2 flat pieces tog, sew around. Lightly stuff and sew in place.

Wing
Make 2

With brown, cast on 10 sts.

Rows 1–12: Knit.

Row 13: [K2tog] across—5 sts.

Cut, leaving long end of yarn. Thread end into yarn needle, draw through all sts on needle, pull tight to secure. Fold in half and sew side seam. Sew in place. ❖

Teddy Bear

Design by Michele Wilcox

Skill Level

 ■■□□ EASY

Size
About 7 inches tall

Materials
- Worsted weight yarn: 2½ oz/125 yds light brown and small amount light gold
- Pearl cotton: Small amount black
- Size 6 (4mm) needles or size needed to obtain gauge
- Polyester fiberfill

 4 MEDIUM

Gauge
14 sts and 24 rows = 4 inches/10cm in St st.
To save time, take time to check gauge.

Special Abbreviation
Knit in front and back (kfb): Inc 1 by knitting in front and back of next st.

Head
Beg at neck, with light brown, cast on 18 sts.

Row 1: Knit.

Row 2: Purl.

Row 3: Kfb in each st across—36 sts.

Row 4: Purl.

Rows 5–20: [Rep Rows 1 and 2] 8 times.

Row 21: [K2tog] across row—18 sts.

Row 22: Purl.

Row 23: Rep Row 21—9 sts.

Cut, leaving long end of yarn. Thread end into yarn needle, draw through all sts on needle and pull tight to secure. Sew back seam and stuff head. Do not sew neck opening.

Ear
Make 2

With light brown, cast on 12 sts.

Rows 1–4: Work in St st.

Row 5: [K2tog] across—6 sts.

Row 6: Purl.

Cut, leaving a long end of yarn. Thread end into yarn needle, draw through all sts on needle and pull tight to secure. Do not stuff. Sew seam and sew bottom edge flat. Sew in place.

Snout
With gold, work as for ear. Do not close bottom edge opening but lightly stuff and sew in place on head. Embroider black satin stitch eyes and nose, and straight stitches for mouth.

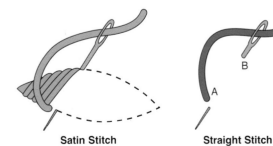

Satin Stitch   Straight Stitch

Tummy

With light gold, cast on 5 sts.

Row 1: Knit.

Row 2: Kfb in each st across—10 sts.

Rows 3–14: Knit.

Row 15: [K2tog] across—5 sts. Bind off.

Body

Beg at bottom of body, with light brown, cast on 12 sts.

Row 1: Knit.

Row 2: Purl.

Row 3: Kfb of each st across—24 sts.

Row 4: Purl.

Row 5: *K3, kfb; rep from * across—30 sts.

Row 6: Purl.

Rows 7–20: Rep [Rows 1 and 2] 7 times.

Row 21: *K3, k2tog; rep from * across—24 sts.

Row 22: Purl.

Row 23: *K2, k2tog; rep from * across—18 sts.

Row 24: Purl.

Row 25: *K1, k2tog; rep from * across—12 sts.

Row 26: Purl.

Cut, leaving long end of yarn. Thread end into yarn needle, draw through all sts on needle and pull tight to secure. Sew back seam and stuff body. Attach tummy and sew bottom seam across. Fit neck over top of body and sew in place.

Arm

Make 2

With light brown, cast on 12 sts.

Row 1: Knit.

Row 2: Purl.

Rows 3–8: Rep [Rows 1 and 2] 3 times.

Row 9: [K2tog] across—6 sts.

Row 10: Purl.

Leg

Make 2

With light brown, cast on 15 sts.

Row 1: Knit.

Row 2: Purl.

Rows 3–10: Rep [Rows 1 and 2] 4 times.

Row 11: [K2tog] 7 times, k1—8 sts.

Row 12: [P2tog] across—4 sts.

Cut, leaving long end of yarn. Thread end into yarn needle, draw through all sts on needle and pull tight to secure. Sew side seam. Stuff and sew in place.

Tail

With light brown, cast on 10 sts.

Rows 1–3: Work in St st.

Row 4: [P2tog] across—5 sts.

Cut, leaving long end of yarn. Thread end into yarn needle, draw through all sts on needle and pull tight to secure. Sew side seam. Stuff and sew in place at bottom of back body seam. ❖

Curious Cat

Design by Michele Wilcox

Skill Level

 EASY

Size
About 7 inches high

Materials
- Worsted weight yarn: 1¼ oz/62 yds each light gold and beige and small amount off-white
- Pearl cotton: Small amount each of green, black and pink
- Size 6 (4mm) needles or size needed to obtain gauge
- Polyester fiberfill

Gauge
14 sts and 24 rows = 4 inches/10cm in St st.
To save time, take time to check gauge.

Special Abbreviation
Knit in front and back (kfb): Inc 1 by knitting in front and back of next st.

Head
Beg at neck, with light gold, cast on 18 sts.

Row 1: Knit.

Row 2: Purl.

Row 3: With beige, kfb in each st across—36 sts.

Row 4: Purl.

Note: Continue in stripe sequence of 2 rows light gold, 2 rows beige.

Rows 5–20: [Rep Rows 1 and 2] 8 times.

Row 21: [K2tog] across row—18 sts.

Row 22: Purl.

Row 23: Rep Row 21—9 sts.

Cut, leaving long end of yarn. Thread end into yarn needle, draw through all sts on needle and pull tight to secure. Sew back seam and stuff head. Do not sew neck opening.

Ear
Make 2

With light gold, cast on 10 sts.

Row 1: Knit.

Row 2: Purl.

Row 3: [K2tog] across—5 sts.

Row 4: Purl.

Cut, leaving long end of yarn. Thread end into yarn needle, draw through all sts on needle and pull tight to secure. Do not stuff. Sew side seam. Flatten and sew in place.

Snout

With white, cast on 20 sts.

Row 1: Knit.

Row 2: Purl.

Row 3: [K2tog] across—10 sts.

Row 4: Purl.

Row 5: [K2tog] across—5 sts.

Row 6: Purl.

Cut, leaving long end of yarn. Thread end into yarn needle, draw through all sts on needle and pull tight to secure. Sew seam. Lightly stuff and sew in place.

Embroider pink satin stitch nose and black straight stitches for mouth and whiskers. Embroider green satin stitch eyes with black satin stitch pupils over center and a black outline on top of eye.

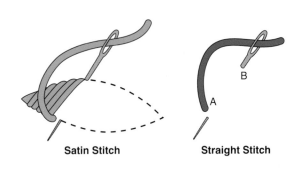

Satin Stitch   **Straight Stitch**

Outline Stitch

Tummy

With beige, cast on 5 sts.

Row 1: Knit.

Row 2: Kfb in each st across—10 sts.

Rows 3–14: Knit.

Row 15: [K2tog] across—5 sts. Bind off.

Body

Beg at bottom of body, with light gold, cast on 12 sts.

Row 1: Knit.

Row 2: Purl.

Row 3: With beige, kfb of each st across—24 sts.

Row 4: Purl.

***Note:** Continue in stripe sequence of 2 rows light gold, 2 rows beige.*

Row 5: With light gold, *k3, kfb; rep from * across—30 sts.

Row 6: Purl.

Rows 7–20: Rep [Rows 1 and 2] 7 times.

Row 21: *K3, k2tog; rep from * across—24 sts.

Row 22: Purl.

Row 23: *K2, k2tog; rep from * across—18 sts.

Row 24: Purl.

Row 25: *K1, k2tog; rep from * across—12 sts.

Row 26: Purl.

Cut, leaving long end of yarn. Thread end into yarn

needle, draw through all sts on needle and pull tight to secure. Sew back seam and stuff body. Attach tummy and sew bottom seam across. Fit neck of head over top of body and sew in place.

Arm
Make 2

With light gold, cast on 12 sts.

Row 1: Knit.

Row 2: Purl.

Note: Work in stripe sequence of 2 rows light gold, 2 rows beige throughout.

Rows 3–8: Rep [Rows 1 and 2] 3 times.

Row 9: [K2tog] across—6 sts.

Row 10: Purl.

Cut, leaving long end of yarn. Thread end into yarn needle, draw through all sts on needle and pull tight to secure. Sew side seam. Stuff arms and sew in place.

Leg
Make 2

With light gold, cast on 15 sts.

Row 1: Knit.

Row 2: Purl.

Note: Work stripe sequence of 2 rows light gold, 2 rows beige throughout.

Rows 3–10: Rep [Rows 1 and 2] 4 times.

Row 11: [K2tog] 7 times, k1—8 sts.

Row 12: [P2tog] across—4 sts.

Cut, leaving long end of yarn. Thread end into yarn needle, draw through all sts on needle and pull tight to secure. Sew side seam. Stuff and sew in place.

Tail
With light gold, cast on 10 sts.

Note: Work stripe sequence of 2 rows light gold, 2 rows beige throughout.

Rows 1–16: Work in St st.

Row 17: [K2tog] across—5 sts.

Row 18: Purl.

Cut, leaving long end of yarn. Thread end into yarn needle, draw through all sts on needle and pull tight to secure. Sew side seam. Stuff and sew in place. ❖

Happy Dog

Design by Michele Wilcox

Skill Level

■■□□ EASY

Size

About 7 inches tall

Materials

- Worsted weight yarn: 2½ oz/125 yds beige and small amount each of red, black and white
- Size 6 (4mm) needles or size needed to obtain gauge
- Polyester fiberfill

Gauge

14 sts and 24 rows = 4 inches/10cm in St st.
To save time, take time to check gauge.

Special Abbreviation

Knit in front and back (kfb): Inc 1 by knitting in front and back of next st.

Head

Beg at neck, with beige, cast on 18 sts.

Row 1: Knit.

Row 2: Purl.

Row 3: Kfb in each st across—36 sts.

Row 4: Purl.

Rows 5–20: [Rep Rows 1 and 2] 8 times.

Row 21: [K2tog] across row—18 sts.

Row 22: Purl.

Row 23: Rep Row 21—9 sts.

Cut, leaving long end of yarn. Thread end into yarn needle, draw through all sts on needle and pull tight to secure. Sew back seam and stuff head. Do not sew neck opening.

Ear

Make 2 (1 beige and 1 black)

Cast on 10 sts.

Row 1: Knit.

Row 2: Purl.

Row 3: *K1, kfb; rep from * across—15 sts.

Row 4: Purl.

Rows 5–10: Rep [Rows 1 and 2] 3 times.

Row 11: [K2tog] 7 times, k1—8 sts.

Row 12: [P2tog] across—4 sts.

Cut, leaving long end of yarn. Thread end into yarn needle, draw through all sts on needle and pull tight to secure. Sew side seam. Lightly stuff and referring to photo, sew in place.

Eye patch

With white, cast on 3 sts.

Row 1: Kfb in each st across—6 sts.

Rows 2–5: Knit.

Row 6: [K2tog] across—2 sts.

Cut, leaving long end of yarn. Thread end into yarn needle, draw through both sts on needle and pull tight to secure.

Eye

Make 2

With black, cast on 2 sts.

Row 1: Kfb of each st—4 sts.

Row 2: [K2tog] twice—2 sts.

Cut, leaving a long end. Thread end into yarn needle, draw through both sts on needle and pull tight to secure. Gather around the edge of piece and pull tog. Sew one black eye in center of eye patch and the other on other side of face. Sew eye patch in place.

Snout Top

With beige, cast on 14 sts.

Rows 1–6: Work in St st.

Row 7: [K2tog] across—7 sts.

Row 8: Purl.

Cut, leaving a long end. Thread end into yarn needle, draw through all sts on needle and pull tight to secure. Sew side seam and stuff. Referring to photo, sew in place on head.

Snout Bottom
With beige, cast on 10 sts.

Rows 1–4: Work in St st.

Row 5: [K2tog] across—5 sts.

Row 6: Purl.

Cut, leaving a long end. Thread end into yarn needle, draw through all sts on needle and pull tight to secure. Sew side seam, stuff and sew in place directly under top snout.

Tongue
With red, cast on 3 sts.

Rows 1–4: Work in St st.

Cut, leaving a long end. Thread end into yarn needle, draw through all sts on needle and pull tight to secure. Sew in place.

Nose
With black, cast on 3 sts.

Row 1: Kfb in each st across—6 sts.

Row 2: Purl.

Row 3: Knit.

Row 4: Purl.

Row 5: [K2tog] across. Bind off.

Gather around edge of piece and pull to tighten, stuffing lightly before you pull tight. Sew in place.

Tummy
With white, cast on 5 sts.

Row 1: Knit.

Row 2: Kfb in each st across—10 sts.

Rows 3–14: Knit.

Row 15: [K2tog] across—5 sts. Bind off.

Body
Beg at bottom of body, with beige, cast on 12 sts.

Row 1: Knit.

Row 2: Purl.

Row 3: Kfb of each st across—24 sts.

Row 4: Purl.

Row 5: *K3, kfb; rep from * across—30 sts.

Row 6: Purl.

Rows 7–20: Rep [Rows 1 and 2] 7 times.

Row 21: *K3, k2tog; rep from * across—24 sts.

Row 22: Purl.

Row 23: *K2, k2tog; rep from * across—18 sts.

Row 24: Purl.

Row 25: *K1, k2tog; rep from * across—12 sts.

Row 26: Purl.

Cut, leaving long end of yarn. Thread end into yarn needle, draw through all sts on needle and pull tight to secure. Sew back seam and stuff. Attach tummy and sew bottom seam across. Fit neck of head over top of body and sew in place.

Arm
Make 2

With beige, cast on 12 sts.

Row 1: Knit.

Row 2: Purl.

Rows 3–8: Rep [Rows 1 and 2] 3 times.

Row 9: [K2tog] across—6 sts.

Row 10: Purl.

Cut, leaving long end of yarn. Thread end into yarn needle, draw through all sts on needle and pull tight to secure. Sew side seam. Stuff and sew in place.

Leg
Make 2

With beige, cast on 15 sts.

Row 1: Knit.

Row 2: Purl.

Rows 3–10: Rep [Rows 1 and 2] 4 times.

Row 11: [K2tog] 7 times, k1—8 sts.

Row 12: [P2tog] across—4 sts.

Cut, leaving long end of yarn. Thread end into yarn needle, draw through all sts on needle and pull tight to secure. Sew side seam. Stuff and sew in place.

Tail

With beige, cast on 10 sts.

Row 1: Knit.

Row 2: Purl.

Row 3: *K1, kfb; rep from * across—15 sts.

Row 4: Purl.

Rows 5 and 6: Rep Rows 1 and 2.

Row 7: With white, knit.

Row 8: Purl.

Row 9: *K1, k2tog; rep from * across—9 sts.

Row 10: Purl.

Row 11: *K1, k2tog; rep from * across—6 sts.

Row 12: Purl.

Row 13: [K2tog] across—3 sts.

Cut, leaving long end of yarn. Thread end into yarn needle, draw through all sts on needle and pull tight to secure. Sew seam. Stuff and sew in place. ❖

Stinky Skunk

Design by Michele Wilcox

Skill Level

 ◼◼☐☐ EASY

Size
About 7 inches tall

Materials
- Worsted weight yarn: 2½ oz/125 yds black and small amount each of white, orange and gold
- Pearl cotton: Small amount each of pink and blue
- Size 6 (4mm) needles or size needed to obtain gauge
- Stitch holders
- Polyester fiberfill

Gauge
14 sts and 24 rows = 4 inches/10cm in St st. To save time, take time to check gauge.

Special Abbreviation
Knit in front and back (kfb): Inc 1 by knitting in front and back of next st.

Head
Beg at neck, with black, cast on 18 sts.

Row 1: Knit.

Row 2: Purl.

Row 3: Kfb in each st across—36 sts.

Row 4: Purl.

Rows 5–20: [Rep Rows 1 and 2] 8 times.

Row 21: [K2tog] across row—18 sts.

Row 22: Purl.

Row 23: Rep Row 21—9 sts.

Cut, leaving long end of yarn. Thread end into yarn needle, draw through all sts on needle and pull tight to secure. Sew back seam and stuff head. Do not sew neck opening.

Snout
With black, cast on 20 sts.

Row 1: Knit.

Row 2: Purl.

Row 3: [K2tog] across—10 sts.

Row 4: Purl.

Row 5: [K2tog] across—5 sts.

Row 6: Purl.

Cut, leaving long end of yarn. Thread end into yarn needle, draw through all sts on needle and pull tight to secure. Sew seam.

With pink pearl cotton, embroider satin stitch nose and 3 straight stitches for mouth. Stuff lightly and sew in place.

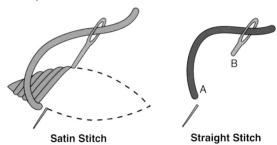

Satin Stitch   Straight Stitch

Embroider blue satin stitch eyes on head above snout.

Ear
Make 2

With black, cast on 10 sts.

Row 1: Knit.

Row 2: Purl.

Row 3: [K2tog] across—5 sts.

Row 4: Purl.

Cut, leaving long end of yarn. Thread end into yarn needle, draw through all sts on needle and pull tight to secure. Do not stuff. Sew side seam. Flatten and sew in place.

Flower
With orange, cast on 3 sts.

Row 1: Knit.

Row 2: Kfb in each st across—10 sts.

Rows 3–14: Knit.

Row 15: [K2tog] across—5 sts. Bind off.

Body

Beg at bottom of body, with black cast on 12 sts.

Row 1: Knit.

Row 2: Purl.

Row 3: Kfb of each st across—24 sts.

Row 4: Purl.

Row 5: *K3, kfb; rep from * across—30 sts.

Row 6: Purl.

Rows 7–20: Rep [Rows 1 and 2] 7 times.

Row 21: *K3, k2tog; rep from * across—24 sts.

Row 22: Purl.

Row 23: *K2, k2tog; rep from * across—18 sts.

Row 24: Purl.

Row 25: *K1, k2tog; rep from * across—12 sts.

Row 26: Purl.

Cut, leaving long end of yarn. Thread end into yarn needle, draw through all sts on needle and pull tight to secure. Sew back seam and stuff. Attach tummy and sew bottom seam across. Fit neck of head over top of body and sew in place.

Tail

With black, cast on 12 sts.

Row 1: Knit.

Row 2: Purl.

Row 3: Kfb in each st across—24 sts.

Row 4: Purl.

Rows 5–8: Rep [Rows 1 and 2] twice.

Row 9: *K2, k2tog; rep from * across—18 sts.

Row 10: Purl.

Row 11: Knit.

Row 12: Purl.

Row 13: *K1, k2tog; rep from * across—12 sts.

Rows 14–16: Rep Rows 10–12.

Row 17: [K2tog] across—6 sts.

Row 2: K3, cast on 3 sts.

Row 3: Knit across 3 cast-on sts, turn.

Row 4: K3, cast on 3 sts.

Rows 5–10: Rep [Rows 3 and 4] 3 times—15 sts.

Row 11: [K2tog] 7 times, k1.

Row 12: [K2tog] across.

Cut, leaving long end of yarn. Thread end into yarn needle, draw through all sts on needle and pull tight to secure. Make gold French knot in center of flower. Sew in place.

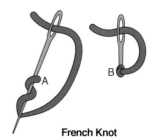

French Knot

Tummy

With beige, cast on 5 sts.

Row 1: Knit.

Cut, leaving long end of yarn. Thread end into yarn needle, draw through all sts on needle and pull tight to secure. Sew seam. Stuff and sew in place.

Arm
Make 2

With black, cast on 12 sts.

Row 1: Knit.

Row 2: Purl.

Rows 3–8: Rep [Rows 1 and 2] 3 times.

Row 9: [K2tog] across—6 sts.

Row 10: Purl.

Cut, leaving long end of yarn. Thread end into yarn needle, draw through all sts on needle and pull tight to secure. Sew side seam. Stuff and sew in place on each side of body.

Leg
Make 2

With black, cast on 15 sts.

Row 1: Knit.

Row 2: Purl.

Rows 3–10: Rep [Rows 1 and 2] 4 times.

Row 11: [K2tog] 7 times, k1—8 sts.

Row 12: [P2tog] across—4 sts.

Cut, leaving long end of yarn. Thread end into yarn needle, draw through all sts on needle and pull tight to secure. Sew side seam. Stuff and sew in place on each side of body beneath tummy.

Stripe
With white, cast on 3 sts.

Row 1: Knit.

Row 2: Purl.

Rows 3–8: Rep [Rows 1 and 2] 3 times.

Row 9: Kfb, knit to last st, kfb—5 sts.

Row 10: Purl.

Row 11: K2, kfb, k2—6 sts.

Rows 12–36: Beg with purl row, work in St st.

Row 37: K3 and place on holder, knit rem 3 sts.

First half stripe
Rows 38–52: Beg with purl row, work in St st on 3 sts, put these 3 sts on holder.

Second half stripe
Row 38: Place 3 sts from first holder on needle and purl across.

Rows 39–52: Beg with knit row, work in St st.

Joined stripe
Row 53: K3, being careful not to twist, place sts from 2nd holder onto LH needle and knit them—6 sts.

Row 54: Purl.

Row 55: K2, k2tog, k2—5 sts.

Rows 56–62: Beg with purl row, work in St st.

Row 63: K2tog, k1, k2tog—3 sts.

Row 64: Purl.

Cut, leaving long end of yarn. Thread end into yarn needle, draw through all sts on needle and pull tight to secure. Pin stripe to body having cast-on sts at center front above snout, half stripes forming circle on back of body and joined stripe on tail. Sew in place. ❖

Nutty Squirrel

Design by Michele Wilcox

Skill Level
 ◼◼☐▱ **EASY**

Size
About 7 inches tall

Materials
- Worsted weight yarn: 2½ oz/125 yds gray and small amount off-white
- Pearl cotton: Small amount black
- Size 6 (4mm) needles or size needed to obtain gauge
- Polyester fiberfill
- 2 small black button eyes (optional)
- 5-inch square of cardboard (for pompom tail)

4 MEDIUM

Gauge
14 sts and 24 rows = 4 inches/10cm in St st.
To save time, take time to check gauge.

Special Abbreviation
Knit in front and back (kfb): Inc 1 by knitting in front and back of next st.

Pattern Note
If animal is to be used by a young child, work optional satin stitch eye instead of adding button eyes.

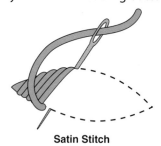

Satin Stitch

Head
Beg at neck, with gray, cast on 18 sts.

Row 1: Knit.

Row 2: Purl.

Row 3: Kfb in each st across—36 sts.

Row 4: Purl.

Rows 5–20: [Rep Rows 1 and 2] 8 times.

Row 21: [K2tog] across row—18 sts.

Row 22: Purl.

Row 23: Rep Row 21—9 sts.

Cut, leaving long end of yarn. Thread end into yarn needle, draw through all sts on needle and pull tight to secure. Sew back seam and stuff head. Do not sew neck opening.

Snout
With gray, cast on 18 sts.

Row 1: Knit.

Row 2: Purl.

Row 3: [K2tog] across—9 sts.

Row 4: Purl.

Cut, leaving long end of yarn. Thread end into yarn needle, draw through all sts on needle and pull tight to secure. Sew seam. Lightly stuff and sew in place.

With black pearl cotton, embroider satin stitch nose and 3 straight stitches for mouth. Sew on button eyes or embroider satin stitch eyes.

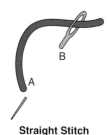

Straight Stitch

Ear
Make 2

With gray, cast on 6 sts.

Row 1: Knit.

Row 2: Purl.

Row 3: [K2tog] 3 times.

Cut, leaving long end of yarn. Thread end into yarn needle, draw through all sts on needle and pull

tight to secure. Sew seam. Sew cast-on edge in half and sew through all thicknesses. Sew in place.

Tummy

With off-white, cast on 5 sts.

Row 1: Knit.

Row 2: Kfb in each st across—10 sts.

Rows 3–14: Knit.

Row 15: [K2tog] across—5 sts. Bind off.

Body

Beg at bottom of body, with gray, cast on 12 sts.

Row 1: Knit.

Row 2: Purl.

Row 3: Kfb of each st across—24 sts.

Row 4: Purl.

Row 5: *K3, kfb; rep from * across—30 sts.

Row 6: Purl.

Rows 7–20: Rep [Rows 1 and 2] 7 times.

Row 21: *K3, k2tog; rep from * across—24 sts.

Row 22: Purl.

Row 23: *K2, k2tog; rep from * across—18 sts.

Row 24: Purl.

Row 25: *K1, k2tog; rep from * across—12 sts.

Row 26: Purl.

Cut, leaving long end of yarn. Thread end into yarn needle, draw through all sts on needle and pull tight to secure. Sew back seam and stuff body. Attach tummy and sew bottom seam across. Fit neck of head over top of body and sew in place.

Arm

Make 2

With gray, cast on 12 sts.

Row 1: Knit.

Row 2: Purl.

Rows 3–8: Rep [Rows 1 and 2] 3 times.

Row 9: [K2tog] across—6 sts.

Row 10: Purl.

Cut, leaving long end of yarn. Thread end into yarn needle, draw through all sts on needle and pull

tight to secure. Sew side seam. Stuff and sew in place.

Leg

Make 2

With gray, cast on 15 sts.

Row 1: Knit.

Row 2: Purl.

Rows 3–10: Rep [Rows 1 and 2] 4 times.

Row 11: [K2tog] 7 times, k1—8 sts.

Row 12: [P2tog] across—4 sts.

Cut, leaving long end of yarn. Thread end into yarn needle, draw through all sts on needle and pull tight to secure. Sew side seam. Stuff and sew in place.

Tail

Cut 250-inch length of gray yarn. Wrap gray 25 times around 5-inch square of cardboard, slide lps off cardboard and tie tightly in center of all lps using 250-inch length of yarn. Rep 5 times more, sewing each new bundle on top of previous bundle(s). When all bundles are complete, cut all lps and trim evenly. Sew tail in place at bottom of back body seam. Attach again about 1-inch from bottom to hold tail up. ❖

Frankie Frog

Design by Michele Wilcox

Skill Level

 EASY

Size

About 7 inches tall

Materials

- Worsted weight yarn: 2½ oz/125 yds green and small amount each of light green, white and black

- Size 6 (4mm) needles or size needed to obtain gauge
- Polyester fiberfill

Gauge

14 sts and 24 rows = 4 inches/10cm in St st.
To save time, take time to check gauge.

Special Abbreviation

Knit in front and back (kfb): Inc 1 by knitting in front and back of next st.

Head

Beg at neck, with green, cast on 18 sts.

Row 1: Knit.

Row 2: Purl.

Row 3: Kfb in each st across—36 sts.

Row 4: Purl.

Rows 5–20: [Rep Rows 1 and 2] 8 times.

Row 21: [K2tog] across row—18 sts.

Row 22: Purl.

Row 23: Rep Row 21—9 sts.

Cut, leaving long end of yarn. Thread end into yarn needle, draw through all sts on needle and pull tight to secure. Sew back seam and stuff head. Do not sew neck opening.

Eye
Make 2

With green, cast on 15 sts.

Row 1: Knit.

Row 2: Purl.

Rows 3 and 4: Rep Rows 1 and 2.

Row 5: [K2tog] 7 times, k1—8 sts.

Row 6: [P2tog] across—4 sts.

Cut, leaving long end of yarn. Thread end into yarn needle, draw through all sts on needle and pull tight to secure. Sew seam.

White of eye
Make 2

With white, cast on 3 sts.

Row 1: Kfb of each st—6 sts.

Row 2: Kfb of each st—12 sts. Bind off.

Cut, leaving long end of yarn. Shape into a circle and sew seam. With black, embroider satin stitch pupil. Sew white eye in place in center of green eye. Lightly stuff green eye and sew in place on top of head.

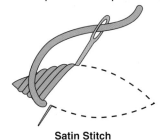

Satin Stitch

Embroider black couching stitch smile on head.

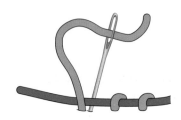

Couching Stitch

Tummy

With light green, cast on 5 sts.

Row 1: Knit.

Row 2: Kfb in each st across—10 sts.

Rows 3–14: Knit.

Row 15: [K2tog] across—5 sts. Bind off.

Body

Beg at bottom of body, with green, cast on 12 sts.

Row 1: Knit.

Row 2: Purl.

Row 3: Kfb of each st across—24 sts.

Row 4: Purl.

Row 5: *K3, kfb; rep from * across—30 sts.

Row 6: Purl.

Rows 7–20: Rep [Rows 1 and 2] 7 times.

Row 21: *K3, k2tog; rep from * across—24 sts.

Row 22: Purl.

Row 23: *K2, k2tog; rep from * across—18 sts.

Row 24: Purl.

Row 25: *K1, k2tog; rep from * across—12 sts.

Row 26: Purl.

Cut, leaving long end of yarn. Thread end into yarn needle, draw through all sts on needle and pull tight to secure. Sew back seam and stuff body. Attach tummy and sew bottom seam across. Fit neck of head over top of body and sew in place.

Thigh
Make 2

Beg at bottom of leg, with green, cast on 6 sts.

Row 1: Kfb of each st across—12 sts.

Row 2: Purl.

Row 3: Kfb of each st—24 sts.

Row 4: Purl.

Rows 5–12: Rep [Rows 1 and 2 of Body] 4 times.

Row 13: [K2tog] across—12 sts.

Row 14: Purl.

Row 15: Rep Row 13—6 sts.

Cut, leaving long end of yarn. Thread end into yarn needle, draw through all sts on needle and pull tight to secure. Sew side seam and stuff. Sew in place on each side of body.

Foot
Make 2

With green, cast on 5 sts for first toe.

Rows 1–3: Knit.

Row 4: Knit across, cast on 5 sts for 2nd toe—10 sts.

Row 5: Knit across 5 cast-on sts only; turn, leaving rem sts unworked.

Rows 6–8: K5. At end of Row 8, cast on 5 sts for 3rd toe.

Row 9: Rep Row 5.

Rows 10–12: K5.

Row 13: Knit across—15 sts.

Row 14: [K2tog] 7 times, k1—8 sts.

Row 15: Knit across. Bind off.

Fold each toe in half and sew seams. Referring to photo, sew in place.

Arm
Make 2

With green [cast on 5 sts, bind off 4 sts, slip last st to LH needle] 3 times for fingers—3 sts on needle.

Row 1: Kfb of each st across—6 sts.

Row 2: Rep Row 1—12 sts.

Row 3: Knit.

Row 4: Purl.

Rows 5–8: Rep [Rows 3 and 4] twice.

Row 9: [K2tog] across—6 sts.

Row 10: Purl.

Cut, leaving long end of yarn. Thread end into yarn needle, draw through all sts on needle and pull tight to secure. Sew arm seam, lightly stuff and sew in place. ❖

Cheepy Chick

Design by Michele Wilcox

Skill Level

◼◼◻◻ EASY

Size
About 7 inches tall

Materials
- Worsted weight yarn: 2½ oz/125 yds white and small amount each of orange, red and black
- Size 6 (4mm) needles or size needed to obtain gauge
- Polyester fiberfill

Gauge
14 sts and 24 rows = 4 inches/10cm in St st.
To save time, take time to check gauge.

Special Abbreviation
Knit in front and back (kfb): Inc 1 by knitting in front and back of next st.

Head
Beg at neck, with white, cast on 18 sts.

Row 1: Knit.

Row 2: Purl.

Row 3: Kfb in each st across—36 sts.

Row 4: Purl.

Rows 5–20: [Rep Rows 1 and 2] 8 times.

Row 21: [K2tog] across row—18 sts.

Row 22: Purl.

Row 23: Rep Row 21—9 sts.

Cut, leaving long end of yarn. Thread end into yarn needle, draw through all sts on needle and pull tight to secure. Sew back seam and stuff head. Do not sew neck opening.

Beak
With orange, cast on 6 sts.

Row 1: Knit.

Row 2: Purl.

Row 3: [K2tog] across—3 sts.

Row 4: Purl.

Cut, leaving long end of yarn. Thread end into yarn needle, draw through all sts on needle and pull tight to secure. Sew seam and referring to photo, sew in place on head.

Wattle
With red, cast on 6 sts.

Rows 1–4: Work in St st.

Cut, leaving long end of yarn. Thread end into yarn needle, draw through all sts on needle and pull tight to secure. Sew seam and sew under beak on head.

Eye
Make 2

With black, cast on 2 sts.

Row 1: Kfb of each st—4 sts.

Row 2: [K2tog] twice—2 sts.

Cut, leaving a long end. Draw end through both sts on needle and pull tightly to secure. Gather around the edge of piece and pull tog. Sew in place on head.

Body
Beg at bottom of body, with white, cast on 12 sts.

Row 1: Knit.

Row 2: Purl.

Row 3: Kfb of each st across—24 sts.

Row 4: Purl.

Row 5: *K3, kfb; rep from * across—30 sts.

Row 6: Purl.

Rows 7–20: Rep [Rows 1 and 2] 7 times.

Row 21: *K3, k2tog; rep from * across—24 sts.

Row 22: Purl.

Row 23: *K2, k2tog; rep from * across—18 sts.

Row 24: Purl.

Row 25: *K1, k2tog; rep from * across—12 sts.

Row 26: Purl.

Cut, leaving long end of yarn. Thread end into yarn needle, draw through all sts on needle and pull tight to secure. Sew back seam and stuff body. Sew bottom seam across. Fit neck of head over top of body and sew in place.

Wing
Make 2

With white, cast on 10 sts.

Rows 1–12: Knit.

Row 13: [K2tog] across—5 sts.

Cut, leaving long end of yarn. Thread end into yarn needle, draw through all sts on needle and pull tight to secure. Fold in half and sew side seam. Sew on each side of body.

Foot
Make 2

With orange, cast on 5 sts for first toe.

Rows 1–3: Knit.

Row 4: Knit across, cast on 5 sts for 2nd toe—10 sts.

Row 5: Knit across 5 cast-on sts only; turn, leaving rem sts unworked.

Rows 6–8: K5. At end of Row 8, cast on 5 sts for 3rd toe.

Row 9: Rep Row 5.

Rows 10–12: K5.

Row 13: Knit across—15 sts.

Row 14: [K2tog] 7 times, k1—8 sts.

Row 15: Knit.

Bind off.

Fold each toe in half and sew seams. Sew to body.

Comb

With red, make 2 pieces same as for foot. Leave flat, do not sew toes.

Holding the 2 flat pieces tog, sew around. Lightly stuff and sew to top of head.

Tail
With white, cast on 10 sts.

Row 1: Bind off 9 sts.

Row 2: Cast on 9 sts.

Row 3: Bind off 9 sts.

Rows 4–13: Rep [Rows 2 and 3] 5 times.

Finish off. Gather ends tog and sew in place. ❖

Precious Pig

Design by Michele Wilcox

Skill Level

 EASY

Size
About 7 inches tall

Materials
- Worsted weight yarn: 2½ oz/ 125 yds pink
- Pearl cotton: Small amounts of red and blue
- Size 6 (4mm) needles or size needed to obtain gauge
- Polyester fiberfill

Gauge
14 sts and 24 rows = 4 inches/10cm in St st.
To save time, take time to check gauge.

Special Abbreviation
Knit in front and back (kfb): Inc 1 by knitting in front and back of next st.

Head
Beg at neck, with pink, cast on 18 sts.

Row 1: Knit.

Row 2: Purl.

Row 3: Kfb in each st across—36 sts.

Row 4: Purl.

Rows 5–20: [Rep Rows 1 and 2] 8 times.

Row 21: [K2tog] across row—18 sts.

Row 22: Purl.

Row 23: Rep Row 21—9 sts.

Cut, leaving long end of yarn. Thread end into yarn needle, draw through all sts on needle and pull tight to secure. Sew back seam and stuff head. Do not sew neck opening.

Snout
With pink, cast on 12 sts.

Row 1: Knit.

Row 2: Purl.

Rows 3–5: Knit.

Row 6: [P2tog] across.

Cut, leaving long end of yarn. Thread end into yarn needle, draw through all sts on needle and pull tight to secure. Sew seam. Lightly stuff and sew in place.

Embroider red pearl cotton couching stitch mouth and blue satin stitch eyes. (See couching stitch illustration on page 22.)

Ear
Make 2

With pink, cast on 12 sts.

Row 1: Knit.

Row 2: Purl.

Row 3: K1, k2tog, k6, k2tog, k1—10 sts.

Row 4: Purl.

Row 5: K3, [k2tog] twice, k3—8 sts.

Row 6: Purl.

Row 7: [K2tog] across—4 sts.

Row 8: Purl.

Cut, leaving long end of yarn. Thread end into yarn needle, draw through all sts on needle and pull tight to secure. Sew seam. Fold top of ear down a little bit, tack in place, if desired. Sew ears in place on head.

Body
Beg at bottom of body, with pink, cast on 12 sts.

Row 1: Knit.

Row 2: Purl.

Row 3: Kfb of each st across—24 sts.

Row 4: Purl.

Row 5: *K3, kfb; rep from * across—30 sts.

Row 6: Purl.

Rows 7–20: Rep [Rows 1 and 2] 8 times.

Row 21: *K3, k2tog; rep from * across—24 sts.

Row 22: Purl.

Row 23: *K2, k2tog; rep from * across—18 sts.

Row 24: Purl.

Row 25: *K1, k2tog; rep from * across—12 sts.

Row 26: Purl.

Cut, leaving long end of yarn. Thread end into yarn needle, draw through all lps on needle and pull tight to secure. Stuff and sew bottom seam across. Fit neck of head over top of body and sew in place.

Legs
Make 4

With pink, cast on 15 sts.

Rows 1–6: Work in St st.

Rows 7–9: Knit.

Row 10: Purl.

Row 11: [K2tog] 7 times, k1—8 sts.

Row 12: [P2tog] across—4 sts.

Cut, leaving long end of yarn. Thread end into yarn needle, draw through all sts on needle and pull tight to secure. Sew side seam. Stuff and referring to photo, sew in place on body.

Tail
With pink, cast on 14 sts.

Row 1: [K2tog] across and bind off at the same time. Finish off and sew to back body seam. ❖

Clothes

Designs by Michele Wilcox

Skill level

 ■■□□ EASY

Size

To fit 7-inch-tall knit animals

Materials

- Sport weight yarn: ½ oz/25 yds each light turquoise, hot pink and lavender and small amount orange and lime green
- Size 3 (3.25mm) needles or size needed to obtain gauge

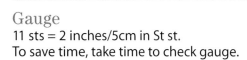

Gauge

11 sts = 2 inches/5cm in St st.
To save time, take time to check gauge.

Special Abbreviation

Knit in front and back (kfb): Inc 1 by knitting in front and back of next st.

Pattern Note

These clothes will fit all the animals.

Scarf

With lavender, cast on 9 sts.

Rows 1 and 2: Knit.

Row 3: K3, p3, k3.

Row 4: P3, k3, p3.

Rows 5 and 6: Rep Rows 3 and 4.

Row 7: Rep Row 3.

Rows 8–10: Knit.

Rows 11–160: Rep [Rows 3–10] 15 times. Bind off.

Sweater

Front/Back

Make 2

With turquoise, cast on 24 sts.

Row 1: K2, p2; rep from * across.

Rows 2–6: Rep Row 1.

Row 7: Knit.

Row 8: Purl.

Rows 9–12: Rep [Rows 7 and 8] twice.

Join lime, do not cut turquoise.

Rows 13 and 14: With lime, knit.

Row 15: With turquoise, knit.

Row 16: Purl.

Rows 17 and 18: With lime, knit. Cut lime.

Row 19: With turquoise, knit.

Row 20: Purl.

Rows 21–28: Rep [Rows 19 and 20] 4 times.

Row 29: Bind off 4 sts, k1, p2, [k2, p2] 3 times, k4—20 sts.

Row 30: Bind off 4 sts, k1, p2, [k2, p2] 3 times; rep from * across—16 sts.

Rows 31–34: Work in k2, p2 rib for collar. Bind off in ribbing.

Sleeve

With turquoise, cast on 24 sts.

Row 1: K2, p2; rep from * across.

Rows 2–6: Rep Row 1.

Bind off in ribbing.

Finishing

Sew neck ribbing and shoulder seams of back and front. Open sweater flat and sew sleeves in place. Sew underarm and side seams.

Skirt

Beg at waist, with hot pink, cast on 48 sts.

Row 1: K2, p2; rep from * across.

Rows 2–6: Rep Row 1.

Row 7: Knit.

Row 8: Purl.

Row 9: Kfb of each st across—96 sts.

Row 10: Purl.

Row 11: Knit.

Row 12: Purl.

Rows 13–16: Knit. Bind off.

Sew back seam.

Hat

With light turquoise, cast on 48 sts.

Row 1: K2, p2; rep from * across.

Rows 2–8: Rep Row 1.

Rows 9–18: Work in St st.

Row 19: *K6, k2tog; rep from * across—42 sts.

Row 20: Purl.

Row 21: *K5, k2tog; rep from * across—36 sts.

Row 22: Purl.

Row 23: *K4, k2tog; rep from * across—30 sts.

Row 24: Purl.

Row 25: *K3, k2tog; rep from * across—24 sts.

Row 26: Purl.

Row 27: *K2, k2tog; rep from * across—18 sts.

Row 28: Purl.

Row 29: [K2tog] across.

Cut, leaving long end of yarn. Thread end into yarn needle and draw through all sts on needle, pull tightly to secure. Sew back seam.

Make a small orange pompom and sew to top of hat. ❖

Knitting Needle Conversion Chart

U.S.	1	2	3	4	5	6	7	8	9	10	10½	11	13	15	17	19	35	50
Continental-mm	2.25	2.75	3.25	3.5	3.75	4	4.5	5	5.5	6	6.5	8	9	10	12.75	15	19	25

Inches into Millimetres & Centimetres

All measurements are rounded off slightly.

inches	mm	cm	inches	cm	inches	cm	inches	cm	inches	cm
⅛	3	0.3	3	7.5	13	33.0	26	66.0	39	99.0
¼	6	0.6	3½	9.0	14	35.5	27	68.5	40	101.5
⅜	10	1.0	4	10.0	15	38.0	28	71.0	41	104.0
½	13	1.3	4½	11.5	16	40.5	29	73.5	42	106.5
⅝	15	1.5	5	12.5	17	43.0	30	76.0	43	109.0
¾	20	2.0	5½	14	18	46.0	31	79.0	44	112.0
⅞	22	2.2	6	15.0	19	48.5	32	81.5	45	114.5
1	25	2.5	7	18.0	20	51.0	33	84.0	46	117.0
1¼	32	3.8	8	20.5	21	53.5	34	86.5	47	119.5
1½	38	3.8	9	23.0	22	56.0	35	89.0	48	122.0
1¾	45	4.5	10	25.5	23	58.5	36	91.5	49	124.5
2	50	5.0	11	28.0	24	61.0	37	94.0	50	127.0
2½	65	6.5	12	30.5	25	63.5	38	96.5		

STANDARD ABBREVIATIONS

[ ] work instructions within brackets as many times as directed

( ) work instructions within parentheses in the place directed

** repeat instructions following the asterisks as directed

* repeat instructions following the single asterisk as directed

" inch(es)

approx approximately

beg begin/beginning

CC contrasting color

ch chain stitch

cm centimeter(s)

cn cable needle

dec decrease/decreases/decreasing

dpn(s) double-point needle(s)

g gram

inc increase/increases/increasing

k knit

k2tog knit 2 stitches together

LH left hand

lp(s) loop(s)

m meter(s)

M1 make one stitch

MC main color

mm millimeter(s)

oz ounce(s)

p purl

pat(s) pattern(s)

p2tog purl 2 stitches together

psso pass slipped stitch over

p2sso pass 2 slipped stitches over

rem remain/remaining

rep repeat(s)

rev St st reverse stockinette stitch

RH right hand

rnd(s) rounds

RS right side

skp slip, knit, pass stitch over—one stitch decreased

sk2p slip 1, knit 2 together, pass slip stitch over the knit 2 together—2 stitches have been decreased

sl slip

sl 1k slip 1 knitwise

sl 1p slip 1 purlwise

sl st slip stitch(es)

ssk slip, slip, knit these 2 stitches together—a decrease

st(s) stitch(es)

St st stockinette stitch/ stocking stitch

tbl through back loop(s)

tog together

WS wrong side

wyib with yarn in back

wyif with yarn in front

yd(s) yard(s)

yfwd yarn forward

yo yarn over

Annie's® *Amigurumi Animal Friends* is published by Annie's, 306 East Parr Road, Berne, IN 46711. Printed in USA. Copyright © 2010, 2014 Annie's. All rights reserved. This publication may not be reproduced in part or in whole without written permission from the publisher.

RETAIL STORES: If you would like to carry this pattern book or any other Annie's publication, visit AnniesWSL.com.

Every effort has been made to ensure that the instructions in this pattern book are complete and accurate. We cannot, however, take responsibility for human error, typographical mistakes or variations in individual work. Please visit AnniesCustomerCare.com to check for pattern updates.

ISBN: 978-1-59217-278-8

14 15 16 17 18